D1549573

DONNA ERICKSON'S

Great Outdoors

FUN BOOK

Illustrated by David LaRochelle

MINNEAPOLIS

*In memory of my uncle Harry A. Sandberg,
who invented extraordinary puzzles and games
and kept the spirit of play alive
throughout his life.*

DONNA ERICKSON'S GREAT OUTDOORS FUN BOOK

Copyright © 1997 Augsburg Fortress. All rights reserved. Except for brief quotations in critical articles or reviews, no part of this book may be reproduced in any manner without prior written permission from the publisher. Write to: Permissions, Augsburg Fortress, 426 S. Fifth St., Minneapolis, MN 55440.

New text copyright © Donna Erickson. New illustrations by David LaRochelle copyright © 1997 Augsburg Fortress. Other text and illustrations reprinted from *Prime Time Together...with Kids* by Donna Erickson, illustrated by David LaRochelle copyright © 1989 Augsburg Fortress; and from *More Prime Time Activities with Kids* by Donna Erickson, illustrated by David LaRochelle, text copyright © 1992 Donna Erickson, illustrations copyright © 1992 Augsburg Fortress.

Cover design by David Meyer
Cover photograph by Ann Marsden

Library of Congress Cataloging-in-Publication Data

Erickson, Donna
    [Great outdoors fun book]
    Donna Erickson's great outdoors fun book / Donna Erickson ; illustrated by David LaRochelle.
        p. cm. — (Prime time family series)
    ISBN 0-8066-3336-0 (alk. paper)
    1. Family recreation. 2. Outdoor recreation. I. LaRochelle, David, ill. II. Title. III. Series.
GV182.8.E75   1997
790.1'91—dc21
                                                            97-1809
                                                            CIP

The paper used in this publication meets the minimum requirements of American National Standard for Information Sciences—Permanence of Paper for Printed Library Materials, ANSI Z329.48-1984.

Manufactured in the U.S.A.   AF 9-3336

01 00 99 98 97   1 2 3 4 5 6 7 8 9 10

What's Inside

Notes from Donna

Outdoor Fun All Year Long

One of my fond memories of childhood is flying kites with my dad. He built box kites, and we tested them on a sandy beach in the Bay Area of San Francisco. Although I can't recall if the kites were airborne for long, I do remember the wonderful feeling of foggy, salty air against my face as I chased clouds and my dad along the shoreline.

Time spent in the great outdoors offers special opportunities for families. The arrival of each season invites us to enjoy the changing colors and temperatures. In spring, we delight in new life emerging from winter's snow and ice. It's a perfect time to help children discover the wonders of nature by starting their own gardens.

During the long days of summer vacation, explore creative ways to beat the heat while you build lasting memories. Plant a **Family Tree** and make a chart to record its growth. Discover how dandelions can be **Wonderful Weeds to Wear**. And on the very hottest days, cool off in your backyard under a **Summer Waterfall Tree**.

When autumn arrives, enjoy a leisurely family walk in the woods, collecting the pinecones and fistfuls of brilliantly colored leaves that carpet the path. Turn these "finds" into a stunning— and lasting—fall centerpiece with suggestions in the **Leaves for Keeps** activity.

Winter can provide outdoor fun, as well. Bundle up and breathe in the frosty air while you build a **Snowball Lamp**, or pack up a winter picnic lunch and set off for an afternoon of **Snow Fun**.

No matter what season it is or where you live, you will discover that this book is full of fresh ideas for family outdoor fun. To help you select activities appropriate to the season, each activity is coded with a symbol for spring (🌷), summer (☀), fall (🍂), or winter (❄). Many of the ideas can be adapted for more than one season, so be creative as you choose.

Remember . . .
it's the little
things that count.
Donna Erickson

Grow It Yourself

Spring in the Air 🌷

Your kids will enjoy watching winter change to spring as they observe new life emerging from the earth and prepare for some grow-it-yourself projects in this section of the book.

To make a "SPRING FIRSTS" calendar, print "Spring comes to _____ " (fill in the name of your city or town) on the top of a sheet of paper. Underneath, write down the month spring arrives in your area. Draw a calendar of the month, making large squares for each day. Hang the poster in your kitchen or family room.

Encourage your kids to be on the lookout for any changes they observe in nature around home, in the neighborhood, or at school. For example, they might note flowers blooming from bulbs (even peeking through the snow), buds on branches, thawing lakes, streams and puddles, fresh smells in the air, and the arrival of robins, nests, and the songs of birds. Mark the sightings on the calendar the day they are discovered. Younger children can illustrate the observations or glue on pictures from magazines.

If your family does some of the spring projects in this book, such as planting seedlings and watching for sprouts, note the observations on the calendar, too.

SPRING COMES TO NORTHFIELD!
APRIL

SUN	MON	TUES	WED	THUR	FRI	SAT
		1	2 ALL THE ICICLES FELL OFF THE ROOF	3	4 DAD DID NOT WEAR HIS WINTER COAT TO WORK	5
6 NEIGHBORS TOOK DOWN CHRISTMAS LIGHTS!	7	8 FIRST RAIN	9 NO MORE SNOW IN THE BACKYARD	10	11 WE PLAYED SOFTBALL AT RECESS!	12 MOM SAW A ROBIN
13 GRASS LOOKS GREEN!	14 BUTTER-FLIES SIGHTED	15	16 I FOUND DANDE-LIONS!	17	18	19
20	21	22	23	24		26
27	28	29	30			

Eggshell Seedlings

You will need: an empty egg carton,
with the top removed
12 eggshell halves
potting soil
flower, vegetable, and herb seeds
felt-tip marker
clear plastic bag, large enough to
hold an egg carton
plastic squeeze bottle
(filled with water)

Give your flower and vegetable gardens a head start by planting seeds indoors. Instead of buying small flower pots, use eggshell halves for small planters. When it's time to grow the young plants outdoors, place them in the soil—eggshell and all. The eggshells provide nourishment to the soil.

Place eggshell halves in the egg carton. Fill each shell two-thirds full with potting soil and plant seeds according to the directions on the package. Label each shell with a felt-tip marker if you wish. Gently water each planted shell using the plastic bottle, then place the egg carton in a plastic bag and set in a dark place. Check the carton every day until the seeds have sprouted. Remove the plastic bag and place the carton in a sunny window. Continue to water the seedlings. Transplant the young plants outside when the danger of frost is over.

Starting a Child's Garden

Kids and dirt seem to have a natural attraction to one another. Why not promote their love for digging in the soil by giving them their own plot in the family garden? This activity will teach them responsibility and provide fun, too.

Stake out a child's special garden

You will need: several white, wood picket-fence sections (available at discount stores and gardening centers)
orange, green, red, and black acrylic paints
one radish and one carrot
knife and fork
craft sticks (one for each kind of plant in the garden)
paper plates (one for each paint color)
small paintbrush
sponge piece
small bedding plants (marigolds, chives, parsley, etc.)
seeds that grow quickly (lettuce, radishes, beans, squash)
gardening tools
watering can
newspaper

Before staking out the garden, let your child decorate the border fence sections. Cover your work surface with newspaper. Then pour a small amount of each color paint onto the paper plates. Cut the carrot and radish in half, lengthwise, and blot dry the cut sides. Stick a fork into the back of the carrot to make a handle. Grip the handle and dip the cut side of the carrot into orange paint. Press the carrot vertically on the pickets. Add carrot tops by dipping the sponge piece into green paint and dabbing lightly at the top of each carrot print. Make radish prints in the same fashion, using red paint. Paint the young gardener's name on the fence, one letter per picket, with black paint. Let the paint dry.

Set aside a space approximately 6 feet x 6 feet for your child's garden. Prepare the soil for planting, then put up the fence along the borders. Assist your beginning gardener with planting.

To make plant markers, paint the names of plants or draw pictures of them on craft sticks. Poke the marker into the ground in the appropriate places.

A Garden on Wheels

You will need: an old wheelbarrow, wagon, or
wagon-like toy on wheels
potting soil
potted vegetables and plants from
a nursery: parsley, beans,
marigolds, pansies, petunias,
begonias, etc.
vegetable or flower seeds: lettuce,
marigolds, nasturtiums
small gardening tools
watering can
ice pick or sharp object

Don't throw away your old wagon or wheelbarrow—it can make a great container for a child's minigarden. This is an easy project for the beginning gardeners in your family, and the results are rewarding. Children can plant, weed, water, and tend their own plants without becoming overwhelmed by a big garden plot. And since the garden is portable, they can move it around the yard or deck for maximum sun exposure.

With an ice pick or other sharp object, an adult should carefully poke drainage holes in the bottom of the wagon or wheelbarrow. Fill it with potting soil. Plant potted plants, keeping in mind their eventual size: put taller plants in the middle, smaller plants along the sides. If there is enough room, help your child plant lettuce seeds in the shape of the first letter of his or her first name.

Water and feed the plants and seedlings frequently.

Plant a Family Tree

Trees give us good things to eat like fruit and nuts, they provide shade, and they become an attractive part of a landscape. Trees are also important air cleaners because they convert carbon dioxide into oxygen. Set aside an afternoon to buy and plant a tree with your child. It's an idea that keeps on growing. Your family will enjoy observing the tree throughout the years with these simple activities.

• Photograph your child standing next to the tree the day it is planted and then one year later. Measure and record the height of your child and the height of the tree each time. Compare heights as the years pass.

• Take a picture of the tree each season.

• Press new leaves and blossoms during the spring, and press changing leaves in the fall.

• Make bark rubbings. Place a piece of paper on the trunk of the tree. Then rub over the paper with the side of a dark crayon. Look at the intricate designs and patterns that appear on the paper.

On a flat work surface, spread out your collection of items from the above activities. Mount them on a large piece of poster board. Write bits of information on the poster to explain the pictures and findings. Frame the poster and hang it on a wall as a reminder of the beauty and wonder of a tree.

Outdoor Arts and Crafts

Fly a Paper-bag Kite!

You will need: paper lunch bag
watercolor or poster paints
colored markers
white household glue
glitter, stickers, magazine pictures, etc.
four 16" streamers of crepe paper or ribbon
string, 20" in length
masking tape

Any time of the year, breezy days offer opportunities for great outdoor family fun. Everyone will enjoy the fresh air and get some exercise when you set aside a weekend afternoon to fly kites. Preschoolers will feel included when they fly their own minikites, made out of paper lunch bags.

When your child celebrates a birthday, making minikites is a fun activity for young party guests. After presents and treats, move the energetic children outside to fly their creations.

Here's how to make a paper-bag kite:

• Decorate the lunch bag with paints or markers. Add stickers, or glue on pictures cut from magazines. For shiny decorations, squiggle glue on the bag and sprinkle glitter on top. Let dry, then shake off excess glitter.

• Glue or tape streamers to the outside bottom corners of the bag.

• For a handle, place the two ends of the string inside the bag, about 1" down from the edge of each side crease. Attach with masking tape.

When the kite is finished, go outside and run with it against the wind. As air fills the bag, the kite stays up and flies.

Just for the Birds

You will need: an empty half-gallon paper
milk carton
small, pointed scissors or cutting tool
5" long, $\frac{3}{16}$" wooden dowel
strong, waterproof glue
small twigs, pieces of bark, moss,
small branches of evergreens
(do not pick these materials off
trees; collect them from the
ground)
1 piece of wire or twine for hanging the
birdhouse

This year, give your feathered friends a new home with this whimsical, easy-to-make birdhouse.

Here's how:

Wash and dry the milk carton. An adult may cut out a circle about 1½ inches in diameter on one of the side panels of the carton, 3 inches above the base. To add a perch for the birds, poke a small hole below the large hole and partially insert the dowel piece.

Close the top of the carton and glue it shut.

Create a natural exterior for the house by covering the carton with "nature finds." For example, arrange and glue twigs evenly across the top of the carton. Cover the walls of the house with bark, moss, and small branches from evergreens.

When the glue is completely dry, poke a hole through the top seam of the carton. Loop wire or twine through the hole, and hang the house from a tree branch or a fence post. Celebrate spring or summer with an "open house" to welcome the birds to the new abode!

Wonderful Weeds to Wear

Warm weather brings families outdoors to enjoy spring and summer pleasures as well as chores. If you have a yard to tend, tackling the weeds is probably on your "to do" list. Once, while working in the garden with my kids, I groaned as I looked at our yard full of dandelions. But when my son happily presented me with a freshly picked bouquet, I was reminded that where an adult might see weeds, a child might see a field of golden flowers.

SLIP
NEXT
STEM
THROUGH
HOLE

Here are some ways to enjoy these die-hard flowers:

• Make crowns and necklaces out of dandelions. Pick a small basketful of the long-stemmed flowers. Slit a hole in one stem with your fingernail or a butter knife, then slip a second stem through it. Make a slit in the second stem and continue the chain until it is as long as you want. Then, attach the last stem to the stem of the first dandelion with a small piece of string. If daisies are growing in your yard or on your patio, add them to the chain, too. Place the crown on your head or around your neck.

• An old superstition says that if you make a wish on a dandelion gone to seed and you are able to blow off all the seeds in one puff, then your wish will come true. Parents may find themselves wishing for a weed-free garden next year!

T-shirt Squirt Art 🌷 ☀ 🍂

You will need: white 100% cotton prewashed
                   T-shirts
              fabric paints in several colors
              several plastic spray bottles
              waxed paper or cardboard
              non-patterned old sheet or
                  large paper tablecloth
              masking tape
              clothesline and clothespins
                  (optional)
              painting shirts
              water

Here's a perfect outdoor party activity for school-age kids. Since the shirts dry in a jiffy, they can be taken home as a party favor at the end of the festivities.

As a backdrop for the activity, hang an old sheet or paper tablecloth on a wall or a clothesline. Insert a piece of cardboard or waxed paper between the two layers of the shirt as protection from any paint that might soak through. Tape or clip the T-shirt to the backdrop.

Pour a different color paint into each squirter. Add water until paint is the right consistency for spraying.

Painters wearing painting shirts to protect clothing should stand about 4 feet from the shirt. Squirt the shirt, one color at a time. When finished with the front, apply paint to the back of the shirt, if you wish. When the painting is complete, remove the shirt from the backdrop and let it dry.

Spray more paint on the backdrop to add to the stray spatters from the project. Let it dry and use it for a colorful, fanciful picnic tablecloth.

Remember to clean the squirters so they won't be clogged when you start your next project.

Note: Iron the shirt on the reverse side if suggested by the paint manufacturer.

Colors from Nature

You will need: a variety of nontoxic plants
and flowers: grass, leaves,
dandelions, geraniums, etc.
crayons or felt-tipped markers
drawing paper

The next time your children are drawing a picture at the picnic table, on your porch, or in your backyard, acquaint them with colors that come from nontoxic growing plants and flowers. Pick some flowers from your garden, choose some blades of grass, add a leaf or two, and rub them on drawing paper to see what colors they make. Experiment with different plants and different colors to make an interesting picture. To emphasize particular objects in your picture, such as trees, flowers, houses, or people, draw an outline with crayons or markers and then fill with nature's colors. Try dandelion yellow, grass green, and geranium pink for starters.

Sunny Hats for Summer Days

You will need: 1 hat or visor
                 squeezable fabric paints
                 sequins, glitter, rhinestones
                 (optional)
                 fabric glue
                 newspaper

We are increasingly aware of the importance of keeping kids' skin protected from the potentially harmful rays of the sun. Applying sunscreen and wearing hats are two things kids can do to protect themselves. Look for inexpensive baseball-style caps and visors in terrific colors in many department and discount stores. Let your kids decorate them with paints, glitter, or sequins, and they'll be more likely to wear them under the summer sun. This project makes a great birthday party activity for preteens, too. They can wear their creations home.

To give the hat support while painting, crumple a piece of newspaper and stuff it inside. Working on a newspaper-covered table, apply the fabric paint. Zigzags, dots, circles, sailboats, fish, watermelon slices, and rainbows are fun and easy to draw. For extra pizzazz, apply glue and sprinkle on sequins, glitter, or rhinestones. If paint is thick, apply the decorations directly onto the paint instead of using glue. Allow paint to dry. Remove the newspaper from the hat.

Leaves for Keeps

You will need: a variety of colorful fall leaves
newspaper
lightweight hammer
large jar
glycerine (available from
drug stores)
warm water

Preserve the beauty of fall leaves the way florists do. It's easy enough for even the youngest child to get involved.

Take a walk together when the leaves are at the height of color, and talk about the changing seasons and the wonders of creation. As you walk, collect the prettiest leaves and small leafy branches you can find. When you return home, spread them out on a newspaper-covered work surface. If the weather is nice, work outdoors on your picnic table. Break apart the ends of the branches or stems by pounding with a lightweight hammer. (This will allow stems to absorb water.) Then, stir together in a jar one part glycerine and three parts warm tap water. Stick the branches and leaves in the mixture, and set the jar on your table as a pretty centerpiece. Within a week you will notice the leaves changing in color and texture. When the leaves have become soft and pliable, remove them from the mixture and use in floral decorations or on a wreath. They will stay pliable.

A Snowball Lamp ❄

You will need: 40 to 50 firm snowballs
votive or pillar candle

This is a favorite winter activity for young children. In your front yard, arrange 12 to 14 snowballs together in a ring shape. Place the candle in the middle of the ring. Add a second ring of 10 to 12 snowballs on top of the first. Continue to pile snowball rings on top, making each ring slightly smaller than the one before until you run out of snowballs. Leave an opening at the top. At sunset, an adult can light the candle for a frosty, warm glow.

Note: Supervise children while burning candles.

Ice Candles ❄

For a small ice candle, you will need:
medium-sized balloon, empty plastic margarine tub, votive candle

For a large ice candle, you will need:
one-gallon plastic ice-cream bucket, vegetable oil, votive candle

Small ice candles

Fill the balloon with water until it is about the size of a softball. Blow once into the balloon and then tie a knot in it. Place the balloon in the margarine tub and set it outside in freezing temperature, or place it in your freezer.

After 4 to 5 hours, a fairly thick shell of ice should form inside the balloon. Check by shaking the balloon gently; if the outside is hard and water can be heard sloshing around inside, it is time to pop the balloon. Discard the balloon. Pour excess water out to form a cavity in the middle. This is where the candle will be placed. Freeze candle holder for 2 more hours, until it is very hard. At sunset, place a votive candle in the center of the ice-candle holder and light it. Place the candle outside by your door to welcome visitors.

USE FAUCET TO FILL BALLOON

ICE SHELL

Large ice candles

Rub a thick coating of vegetable oil on the inside of the ice-cream pail. Fill the pail with water and place it outside in the freezing temperature, or place the pail in the freezer. When the water is partially frozen (after 4 to 5 hours), scoop out a cavity in the middle and insert a votive candle. When the ice is frozen solid, remove it from the ice-cream pail. At sunset, light the candle and place it outside. To store candles when the weather warms up, place them in your freezer.

SCOOPED OUT CAVITY FOR CANDLE

Note: Always supervise children when burning candles.

Backyard Fun and Games

Water Painting for Preschoolers

You will need: clean paintbrushes
empty paint pail or plastic bucket
one-step booster stool
painter's caps (one per child)
soap and water

The next time your preschooler wants to "help"—as in wash the car or paint the garage door with you—try these "painting" ideas. They will give you a chance to spend time with your child and get some projects done, too.

When you are painting, fill an empty paint can or pail with water. Give your kids clean paintbrushes, put painter's caps on their heads, and watch them enjoy "water painting" the side of the house. The water makes the paint on the house look a different color until it dries. Use one-step booster stools so toddlers have a "ladder," too.

When you are washing the car, fill a bucket with suds and water. Children can paint the soapy water on the car—they might especially like to work on the tires.

Just for fun: When your kids say they have nothing to do, suggest they take a paintbrush, dip it into some mud, and draw pictures or write words on the sidewalk. It can be hosed off later or erased with the next rain shower.

Backyard Golf 🌷 🌼 🍃

You will need: empty coffee cans in various sizes,
                drain gutters, boxes, bricks, logs,
                cans, flower pots, sheets of plas-
                tic and sand, long, flat boards,
                and other suitable items
            a bucket of water
            sticks or dowels 2 feet long,
                one for each hole
            construction paper or fabric
            index cards, one for each player
            black felt-tipped marker
            golf balls and golf clubs (real or toy)

Golf is great fun for children and adults. Your family and friends will enjoy this version of the sport right in your own backyard.

Use the coffee cans for "holes" by laying them on their sides. Space the cans around the yard to make a mini-course. Mark each hole with a flag made from a stick or dowel with a triangle of construction paper or fabric attached. Number each flag with a black marker and stick one into the ground next to each can.

Make each hole unique and challenging by arranging your building materials in different configurations. For example, make an incline with a board and a log, and place a container filled with water at the end of the board to make a water hazard. Or, dump sand from the sandbox on a sheet of plastic to create a sand trap.

Once your course is complete, gather real or toy golf clubs (younger players can use a plastic baseball bat) and golf balls. Play in teams and keep track of the score on homemade score sheets made of index cards.

Sidewalk Chalk Talks 🌷 ☀️ 🍂 ❄️

One summer, new hopscotch lines were painted on our school playground to renew interest in a traditional game that requires only an extra skip in your step and a stone to mark the spot.

Playground fun soon spilled over onto our driveway and sidewalk when we bought a bucket of sidewalk chalk in a rainbow of colors.

Here are fun things to do with sidewalk chalk and free time:

• Draw a tic-tac-toe playing board. Use rocks and sticks for markers, or draw "X"s and "O"s with chalk in the spaces.
• Welcome visitors to your home with special greetings on the front walkway and steps.
• Draw an imaginary city on a wide driveway. Make the roads broad enough to accommodate your preschooler's tricycle and push toys.
• Create an imaginary minireplica of your own neighborhood: streets, houses, stores, parks, etc. Youngsters will enjoy pretend games in which they "drive" tricycles or skateboards home from "work," waving to friends and stopping at "stores" to pick up "groceries."

On any given day, the driveway or sidewalk can be transformed into a small world full of adventure, intrigue, and fun that will stimulate any child's imagination.

Always Blowing Bubbles

Catch your kids off guard by inviting them to do something at night that you normally do during the day. One delightful activity is blowing bubbles, especially under the light of a full moon. But, if it's too dark, turn on your porch light, blow the bubbles near a lamppost, or shine a flashlight on them. If the temperature is below zero, bundle up and enjoy blowing bubbles like you've never seen before! You'll be surprised how the bubbles appear motionless at times. Sometimes they bounce when they hit the snow. Watch the bubbles sparkle as they freeze.

To make supper bubbles: Use plastic six-pack beverage holders, biscuit cutters, straws, and funnels. Dip the bubble makers into your bubble brew and either blow through them or wave them in the air.

For homemade bubbles: In an unbreakable container, stir together 1 cup Joy liquid washing detergent, 2 cups warm water, 3 to 4 tablespoons glycerine (available at drugstores), and 1 teaspoon of sugar.

Cool Games for Hot Days ☀

Whether you're organizing a family reunion at a lake, a birthday party picnic in the park, or just some family fun in your backyard, summer heat can affect even the best-planned event. Pages 42 through 47 describe three great game ideas to ensure a cool time despite the heat.

Ice meltdown

You will need: two or more players
one ice cube per player
(for older kids and adults, larger chunks of ice made pint-size milk cartons are especially fun)

The object of the game is to see who can melt his or her ice cubes first. The ice must be touching the player's body at all times until it's completely melted. But you can't put it in your mouth!

43

"Water-Ball" Sports ☀

Wading pool kickball

You will need: eight or more players, barefoot
and in bathing suits
three small, plastic, inflatable
wading pools filled with
water
a sturdy plastic kickball

Place the wading pools at first, second, and
third base. Divide into teams and assign positions. Play normal kickball, except make slides
and splashes in the pools as you run from base
to base.

Water balloon volleyball

You will need: two or more players
one volleyball or badminton net
water balloons

Toss a water balloon from one side of the net
to the player(s) on the other side. The object is
to see how many times the water balloon can
be thrown over the net without breaking.
Discard popped balloons and balloon pieces
properly.

A Summer Waterfall Tree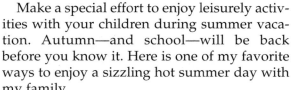

Make a special effort to enjoy leisurely activities with your children during summer vacation. Autumn—and school—will be back before you know it. Here is one of my favorite ways to enjoy a sizzling hot summer day with my family.

Hang a garden hose with a spray nozzle from a tree branch or over a clothesline in your backyard. Tie it in place with rope or heavy twine. Set a wading pool underneath, turn the water on, and let your own family waterfall cool you down. Place lawn chairs around the pool and, when you've stepped out of your waterfall, sit back and sip ice-cold, slushy lemonade together.

Recipe: Squeeze 4 lemons. Pour the juice into a blender with ½ cup of sugar, 1½ cups of water, and a handful of ice cubes. Blend until smooth.

Snow Fun ❄

For people who live in colder climates, winter can seem to last a lifetime. Here are some ideas to help ease "cabin fever."

Play in the snow indoors. FIll your bathtub or a large plastic container with snow. With mittens on their hands, your kids can make sculptures, tunnels, and houses in the snow using sandbox toys, measuring cups, and plastic kitchen utensils.

Study snowflakes. Observe the intricate patterns of freshly fallen snowflakes Sherlock Holmes-style. Simply tape or glue a piece of black velveteen, velvet, or felt on a small, flat piece of cardboard. Refrigerate the piece for a while. Then hold the cloth outside as the snow falls. Once you catch a few flakes on the cloth, observe them immediately with a magnifying glass.

Make a snow angel. This is a perennial favorite! Lie on your back in the snow. Wave your arms up and down and move your legs back and forth. Stand up to see the angel shape.

Enjoy a snowbank picnic. Whether your outing is skating on a frozen pond, snowshoeing in the woods, or cross-country skiing at a nature reserve, bring along a simple picnic to enjoy. When it's time to eat, spread out a blanket in a sunny area and gather your outdoor enthusiasts for a cozy meal. Everyone can savor a bowl of hot chili served with crusty bread, hot chocolate, tea, or coffee. For dessert, bring along citrus fruit or cookies with dates, raisins, and nuts.

Around the Neighborhood

Neighborhood Parade

For a neighborhood parade that's lots of fun, gather kids of all ages on your block or in your apartment building. Decorate bikes, trikes, in-line skates, and wagons. Wear a funny hat and strike up the band!

Here are some ideas to stage the high-spirited event:

• Make and deliver fliers to announce the parade. (A weekend parade often works best because more people are able to attend.) Designate a place where youngsters can bring their bikes for a pre-parade decorating party. Tie ribbons, streamers, and flags to bikes and wagons. Make signs and banners.

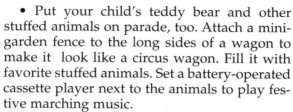

• Put your child's teddy bear and other stuffed animals on parade, too. Attach a mini-garden fence to the long sides of a wagon to make it look like a circus wagon. Fill it with favorite stuffed animals. Set a battery-operated cassette player next to the animals to play festive marching music.

• Teens will enjoy participating, too. They can hand out brochures along the parade route or wear sandwich boards advertising their services for mowing lawns, baby-sitting, etc.

• For even more fun, make the day a real picnic and top off the event with a potluck meal or ice-cream social. Your driveway, yard, or a nearby park can be the gathering spot. If you have a meal, each family should bring along plates, utensils, beverages, plus a main dish, salad, or dessert to share.

• For a dessert bar, set up big tubs of ice cream on a picnic table. Ask families to bring their favorite toppings.

Junior Garage Sale 🌷 ☀ 🍂 ❄

Planning and running your next family garage sale can be more than a money-making venture for your kids.

Dollars may be the incentive for parting with their toys, books, and games, but along the way they'll also reap the benefits of hands-on experience in marketing, merchandising, and sales.

Here are some tips to help your kids recycle —the garage-sale way:

• Set aside time one or two weeks before the sale to help your kids sort through their books, toys, games, and outgrown clothes. Wash any items that are soiled.

• Put stickers on each of the items and price them to sell.

• Although you may advertise the family sale in the newspaper, your kids can make their own fliers to distribute to friends and neighbors.

• Make a big poster with "EXTRAORDINARY KID-STUFF" printed in large letters to display in the kids' department of the sale.

• On the day of the sale, provide a table for the kids to display their wares. Items may be sorted by category: sports equipment, costumes, action figures, etc.

• Find a cash box and be sure someone is always in charge of it.

• Be prepared to bargain, especially on the price of bikes, scooters, and skates.

• At the end of the sale, gather the leftover items that are in good condition, remove the price stickers, and donate the leftover items to a nonprofit organization.

Welcome New Kids to Your Block

When a family moves into your neighborhood, you and your children can help the new kids feel like part of the community with a welcome-wagon greeting.

Here's how:

Decorate a wagon or wheelbarrow with streamers and balloons, and attach a "WELCOME TO OUR NEIGHBORHOOD" sign. (If you don't have a wagon or wheelbarrow, decorate a big, empty box instead.) Then fill your "welcome wagon" with items such as:

• Cookies served on a plate. Cookies made with a cookie cutter in the shape of your state are especially fun.

• A list of reliable baby-sitters.

• A schedule of sporting events, outdoor concerts in nearby parks, and other community events.

• Coupons for a favorite local pizza restaurant.

- Names, pictures, phone numbers, and addresses of neighborhood kids.
- A map of the neighborhood that indicates important landmarks, such as the community swimming pool, beaches, bike paths, churches, the public library, elementary school, baseball field, skating rink, and so on.
- Copies of your local newspaper.

Sounds of the Neighborhood

You will need: tape recorder
                several blank tapes

Kids are born collectors. You've probably already observed their inclination to save rocks, sticks, shells, and marbles. Here's an idea for a novel collection: record and save neighborhood sounds.

Armed with a loaded cassette recorder, kids can spend hours capturing the sounds that surround them—a neighbor's barking dog, an airplane overhead, the newspaper landing on the front porch, birds chattering in a tree, or friends skating past. In the process, they will be sharpening the important skill of careful listening. Once they've filled one tape, they can play it back, pressing the pause button between sounds while the rest of the family tries to identify voices, neighborhood noises, and other sounds.

Here are a few "sound" idea starters:

- a squeaky garage door
- neighbors calling their dogs
- birds in a nearby tree
- the ice-cream wagon
- snow shoveling
- voices of neighbors chatting
- laughter of family and friends
- musical instruments being played
- young children singing favorite songs
- the next-door neighbor's old car

Summer Camp at Home ☀

Listening to the tall tales of older siblings or cousins who have been to camp during the summer can make the younger ones in your family wish for their own adventure. Here are a few fun ideas just for them, to create a pint-size summer camp without leaving home.

• Pitch a small tent in the backyard or drape a big sheet over a picnic table or card table. A large appliance box is also a great find. Lay it flat so the kids can paint the outside in bright colors, adding designs, pictures, and a special name for their summer house. An adult should cut out the windows and doors. Your preschoolers will love to pretend in their own hideaway.

• Make binoculars to spot birds, squirrels, butterflies, and bugs. Glue two bathroom tissue tubes together along the sides. Paint the tubes with poster paint and tie on string so the binoculars can be worn around your child's neck.

For extra fun, play safari. Hide stuffed animals or plastic toys behind shrubs, trees, and planters. Your kids will enjoy searching for them with their play binoculars.

1. Block Party Art Fair— Preparations

You will need: art projects gathered from the children in your area
construction paper for making tickets, or a purchased roll of tickets
paper for posters and fliers
clothesline and clothespins
butcher paper
crayons or felt-tipped markers
cookies, lemonade, popcorn
paper cups and napkins
cashier's box with extra change
face paints (optional)
balloons and streamers
tape player and music cassettes
card tables or picnic tables (for display purposes)

☆ ART FAIR ☆
SAT. JUNE 22
11:00 to 2:00
2578 Sunbow Lane
(Debbie's House)

Are you wondering what to do with all the art projects your children have brought home from school that are overflowing from your closets and refrigerator door? Consider holding a neighborhood art fair. You can even sell the masterpieces at reasonable prices, along with refreshments, and donate the money to a local charity or community organization.

This activity is a great way to get to know your neighbors and build community spirit, too. Contact other parents on your block and set up activities they wish to help with: setting up displays, working at the fair, cleaning up, making posters, providing refreshments, face painting, putting on puppet shows—the more the merrier! Then, gather all the art projects you can find and encourage neighbors to do the same.

Publicize the fair with posters or photocopied fliers the children make with the time, place, and date on them. (A good time is between 4 P.M. and 7 P.M., or on a weekend, so many people will be available to attend.)

2. Block Party Art Fair— The Big Day

On the day of the fair, set up displays, in the front yard, in your driveway, or on your deck or porch (depending on the size of the fair and the weather). String clothesline between trees and poles, and hang paintings, drawings, and some crafts with clothespins. Display sculpture, jewelry, painted rocks, and the like on a picnic table or card table. Set up the refreshments center and a ticket sales booth. You may wish to include a "Permanent Collection" display of artwork that will not be offered for sale. Decorate the area with streamers and balloons, and play music to liven up the atmosphere. Put up posters at places where entertainment and face painting will take place. For toddlers, roll out a long sheet of butcher paper on the ground and place crayons or colored markers next to the paper. The little Picassos can doodle while the older kids enjoy participate in other activities.

As people arrive at the fair, they may purchase tickets to be used for buying treats, purchasing art, face painting, and viewing performances. When the fair is over, have designated helpers clean up, return unsold art, and count the proceeds. Decide on a charity or community service that would benefit from the money, and deliver it with several of the children. Submit a photo or two of the event to your community newspaper—the event just might appear in print.

PERMANENT
COLLECTION

Parents' Page

Healthy Habits for the Great Outdoors

Make health and fitness a family priority as you build outdoor activities into your time together. Here are ideas to promote a healthy lifestyle for the whole family.

• Great days begin with breakfast. Kids and adults can get more out of the fresh air and exercise when they've eaten a good breakfast first. My kids love to smear low-fat cream cheese on a whole-wheat bagel and top it off with tasty, nutritious slices of strawberries, kiwi, applies, and grapes.

• Eat your veggies. Plan your backyard gardens around healthy foods, like lettuce, sweet beans, or carrots. Add tomatoes, green peppers, onions, and oregano to the plot for the makings of a mouthwatering pizza.

• Get in shape together. Teach one another school playground games, such as hopscotch and jump rope. Or find an easy-to-follow nature trail and let your children be the guides.

• Drink water. When you take a break from your outdoor activities, water is the easiest way to quench your thirst. Instead of soda pop or flavored drinks high in sugar, mix fruit concentrates with sparkling water for a healthy energy boost.

• Mark your progress. Make a record of your family's fitness activities on a large sheet of poster board. Across the top, list favorite activities, such as skating, biking, or swimming. Each time you enjoy an outdoor activity, write the date and memorable anecdotes under the appropriate column. You'll create a fun record of your activities and a reminder that family fitness is fun!